Tess McCabe has been working in graphic design, brand management and marketing for most of this century. With both sides of the brain working in harmony, she has the uncanny ability to recognise how to use knowledge and processes to work creatively smarter, not harder. Having run her own graphic design consultancy for over 17 years — as well as a homewares brand, a podcast, a publishing house and non-profit organisation alongside it — she has encountered from both sides the challenges solo operators and bootstrapping businesses face when trying to 'do it all'. Empowering people with information to make their DIY marketing and design ventures easier and more effective — while making the world more aesthetically pleasing in the process — is her goal.

tessmccabe.com.au

Graphic Design Speak was first published in 2013.

Revised edition published 2019 by Creative Minds

A catalogue record for this book is available from the National Library of Australia at catalogue.nla.gov.au

Design and illustrations by Tess McCabe for Creative Minds
'Still Life Of A Mandarin' image by Karina Sharpe: stocksy.com/karinasharpe

ISBN 9780994627353

CREATIVE MINDS
creativemindshq.com

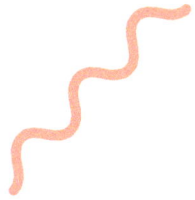

Graphic Design Speak

TIPS, ADVICE
AND JARGON
DEFINED FOR
NON-GRAPHIC
DESIGNERS

Tess McCabe

Contents

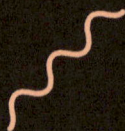

If you have built castles in the sky, your work need not be lost.

Now, put the foundations under them.

HENRY DAVID THOREAU

Introduction

Each industry has its own language, concepts and specialised terms which will be intuitive to insiders, and graphic design is no different. For design professionals, this vocabulary of pixels, Lorem Ipsum and typography is second nature, but can cause those outside of the industry to glaze over with a look of bewilderment.

I have been working professionally as a graphic designer for over 15 years, creating brand logos, marketing material, books, reports, presentations, websites, apps, and all manner of print and digital communications materials. In this time, I regularly encountered people overwhelmed by requests from graphic design professionals to provide high-resolution images or vector files, define their logo's Pantone colour or decide whether they want a DL or A5-size brochure.

Working with my own clients, I try to define graphic design terms as simply as I can, so that what I am asking for is readily understood. And after our project comes to a close, armed with some graphic design knowledge, my clients are able to more confidently field similar requests in the future.

Graphic Design Speak is about explaining, simply, the terms which frequently garner the response: 'Huh? What does that mean?'. My aim is to give you a working knowledge of the words and concepts graphic designers, photographers, web designers and printers commonly use, without explaining the history of graphic design or overloading you with technical talk that you don't need.

Parts One and Two explain in layperson's terms some common areas of graphic design technology and terminology that can cause confusion. Colour, paper sizes, fonts, file types, image sourcing and resolution are all covered. These chapters will hopefully help fill the gaps in your knowledge and provide a grasp of some of the key technical aspects of creating usable, sustainable graphic design outcomes—whether you're DIYing your design, working with a professional, or a combination of both.

Keep this book handy as a reference guide for some of the terminology graphic designers might throw at you. Speaking the same language is key to any successful relationship, and having an understanding of a broad selection of common terms and concepts will assist you to confidently brief and provide feedback to your designer, printer, or other service provider in the name of a swift and efficient collaboration.

And speaking of collaborative experiences, if and when you choose to engage a professional designer, Part Three will help you navigate issues such as briefing, contracts, communication, and what to do in sticky situations. Think of it as a kind of instruction manual, and use as directed (actual results may vary).

If you run your own creative small business, or need to engage a graphic designer for a special project, all of the enclosed information is 'good to know'. (And hey, if you ever happen to be on Who Wants To Be a Millionaire and you're asked 'What do the letters CMYK stand for?', you can answer confidently and pocket that quick cash. Bonus!)

PART ONE

Understanding the language of graphic design

Basic colour terms explained

Colour is undoubtedly a major player in the graphic
designer's communication toolkit. It can define a mood,
become synonymous with a brand, or convey important
information in its own right. But the presentation of
colour in various environments—and how one talks about
producing those colours—is a bevy of acronyms and codes.
Consider this chapter your Rosetta Stone.

RGB
What does it mean?
RGB stands for Red, Green and Blue. Millions of colours can
be made by using different percentages of these three colours.
However, the element that distinguishes RGB from CMYK
(see page 6), is light. The R, G and B are basically coloured
light sources, which is why RGB is used when talking about
on-screen colour (e.g. computer and TV). Zero light = black,
and maximum light = white. Every other colour is in between.
The amount of light emitted to make a certain colour can
be described in a number of different ways (percentages,
fractional values etc), but the most common is integers
(remember them from high school?) between 0 and 255.

Where do you use it?
You use it when talking about colours used on an electronic/
digital screen or device.

The upside

If you're just dealing with the web and documents made to view online, colours are generally specified as RGB. However, just to confuse things, most laser and inkjet printers that you might use at home will print RGB images.

The downside

You can't print professionally if your document is in RGB colour mode. Microsoft Office products specify colour as RGB because they are not programs in which to design things that will be professionally printed using CMYK/Pantone colours, such as books, annual reports, brochures and the like.

Also, because all computer monitors are calibrated differently and emit light in different ways, what you see on-screen can differ from what your neighbour sees, and might not accurately represent what the final printed product will look like.

How is it specified?

RGB colours are specified by their integer number e.g.

R=235, G=152, B=186 and often written like this:
R235 / G152 / B186.

Hex codes are also a way to specify an RGB colour.

Hex codes

Once upon a time, computer monitors only showed green text on a black screen. As technology developed, more colours could be shown on screen, and somewhere along the line, 'they' decided there were 256 colours that every computer monitor could accurately detect. For ages, web designers were told →

→ to use only those 256 'web-safe colours' so their designs would look the same on any computer monitor. However, techonology is advancing so fast that this rule is not really something to be concerned about too much anymore.

Where do you use it?
Hex codes are useful when referencing solid RGB colours in an electronic/digital environment. Similar to RGB, you wouldn't specify a hex code to a printer, but you would to a designer creating graphics that will only be viewed onscreen.

How is it specified?
Hex codes are made up of a hashtag (#) followed by six letters and/or numbers, a combination of numerals 0–9 and letters a–f.

CMYK

CMYK is also known as …
Four-colour, Full-colour, Process colour.

What does it mean?
CMYK stands for Cyan, Magenta, Yellow and Key (Key means black). Millions and millions of different colours can be made using percentages of these four standard colours.

Where do you use it?
CMYK most often refers to colours that are printed on paper.

The upside
You can print almost every colour in the rainbow using CMYK, which means it's great for photos and designs that have lots of colours. It used to be expensive, but printing in CMYK is getting cheaper all the time.

The downside

Some colours can appear dull when printed in CMYK as opposed to those printed with Pantone inks (orange is one example). Also, it can be difficult to match CMYK colours across various products if they have been printed at different times by different printers: the robin egg blue you love might look a bit purple on your business card, and a bit green on your swing tag. There are also some colours that you just can't make using the percentages of CMYK, such as fluorescent and metallic colours (that's when you might consider printing in Pantone—see below).

How is it specified?

CMYK colours are specified by percentages, e.g. C=2%, M=52%, Y=2%, K=1% and often written like this: C2 / M52 / Y2 / K1.

Pantone

Pantone is also known as ...

PMS (Pantone Matching System) or spot colour.

What does it mean?

Pantone is a company. They developed a colour matching system that, although one of many, is the most widely used by graphic designers and printers in Australia.

Pantone colours, unlike CMYK colours, are essentially 'pre-mixed' before they are printed. They are often bolder and brighter than colours mixed by the CMYK percentage system. Fluorescent and metallic colours are amongst the thousands of Pantone colours available.

Where do you use it?

Sometimes you'll want a certain colour to really stand out on a printed item, or for it to be represented more accurately across a few different printed products. Corporations can be very particular about their corporate colours. Remember how a certain chocolate company wanted exclusive rights to a certain shade of purple? You can bet they use a Pantone colour to ensure that purple looks exactly the same each time it's printed. Printing only in Pantone limits your colour choice but can provide a nice creative challenge for a designer.

The upside
You can add Pantone colours to a CMYK/full-colour printed item to ensure a brighter or more accurate feature colour across multiple printed items. 'Special' colours such as fluorescent and metallic can also be printed using Pantone inks.

The downside
You can't print a colour photo (for example) in all-Pantone inks just to make it brighter.

How is it specified?
Every Pantone ink has a specific number attached (like Pantone 123), with a few exceptions that have actual names (like Pantone Warm Red). The 'C' or 'U' which appears after a Pantone name identifies whether the paper being used is coated or uncoated (which can change the intensity and appearance of a Pantone colour when printed).

One-colour

This is also known as ...
Monocolour or single-colour.

What does it mean?
The 'colour' usually references a single Pantone colour, or can also refer to black, which is not technically a Pantone colour but is often paired with them.

Where do you use it?
Traditionally, one-/two-/three-colour print jobs were

cheaper than printing in CMYK. This is not the case so much now, unless you're printing a very high volume, for example thousands of copies. Back before full-colour printing became much more economical, you might have printed in limited colours to keep printing costs down.

The upside
Working with a limited colour range does force a designer to get creative with their colour choice. As mentioned earlier, limiting a colour palette to one or two colours used to be an economical printing choice, so nowadays this approach can help give design projects a retro look.

The downside
Everything on the page has to be printed in tones of the Pantone colours you have chosen.

How is it specified?
Single colours are specified as per Pantone colours.

Duotones and tritones

Also known as
Two-colour or three-colour.

What does it mean?
Designing and printing in duotone or tritone via Pantone colours was once an economic choice, and a way of adding more than one colour to a document without the expense of printing in full colour (CMYK). Depending on which colours were chosen, the Pantone inks could be mixed to produce an array of tones.

Where do you use it?
In print.

How is it specified?
Colours are specified as Pantone colours.

Greyscale

Greyscale is also known as ...
Black and white or B&W.

What does it mean?
A greyscale image is simply another term for a black-and-white image or an image that has many shades of black, white and grey and no other colours.

Where do you use it?
You use it in black-and-white publications.

The upside
Printing entire documents in greyscale can reduce printing costs in comparison to printing in CMYK/full-colour.

The downside
Not every image looks good converted from colour to black and white, and there can be printing issues if an image is very dark.

How is it specified?
The image's colour mode is converted to Greyscale in a program such as Adobe Photoshop.

CMYK

PANTONE

RGB

MONOTONE

DUOTONE

GREYSCALE

Common file types and where to use them

There are many different image file types. In almost any computer program, hit Save As and the drop down menu under the File Name bar will reveal many formats that are relevant only to that particular file type. There are hundreds in total, some are interchangeable for different situations, and some are very specific to the application they are destined for.

How can I tell what type of file it is?

File types are generally determined by their extension, which is the group of letters after the full stop in a file name, for example:

- Image.jpg
- Image.tif
- Words.doc
- Words_and_images.pdf

The filename extensions tell you what type of file the image is, and sometimes, which computer program the file was created in or will open with.

What if the file doesn't have an extension?

If you receive or create a file that is simply called, for example, 'image' and it does not have a file name extension, try right-clicking or double-clicking the image and finding its Properties (PC) or More Info (Mac). The information contained there might tell you.

Can I change the file type by typing in a new extension?

Unfortuntately, you can't turn a JPG into a TIF by just typing over the letters with a new extension name. A file needs to be re-saved with the required extension via the appropriate computer program.

Common file types

JPEG: use in print or on the web

JPEGs are a pretty versatile file format, and the most commonly accepted file across different computers, computer programs, in print and online. JPEGs can be CMYK, RGB, high-resolution or low-resolution. You'd need to do some sleuthing to find out the details of each image. If you're wanting to attach an image to an email and hope its recipient will be able to see it without any trouble, make it a JPEG. The extension for JPEG images can be .jpg and .jpeg depending on what sort of computer the image was originally saved on.

GIF: use on the web

GIF files are never high-resolution and don't print professionally because they are a website-only file type. They are commonly used for images with a few flat colours, shapes and lines like logos. They are not usually suitable for photographic images, as the detail of a photo can become quite pixellated. You can have transparent elements in a GIF. You can also make simple animations with the GIF format. If you want to see animated GIFs in action and have an hour to spare, I recommend searching the term 'kitten animated GIF' online.

PNG: use on the web

PNG files are not usually high-resolution and don't print professionally because they're a website-only file type. They can be used for photographs or for flat-coloured logos, and can be thought of as a superior GIF file. You can have transparent elements in a PNG and often the file size is smaller than for GIFs.

PDF: use to ensure anyone can open the file

PDFs can be created from almost any computer program. The idea behind PDFs (or Portable Document Format) is that anyone with Adobe Reader (a free computer program you can download online) can open and view the PDF, no matter what program the original file was created in.

PDFs are useful like that. Nowadays PDFs can usually also be viewed through an internet browser, so you can view them on your smartphone, too.

TIF: use them in print

A TIF file is usually high-resolution, but you'll need to check. TIFs are good for photographic images or logos, but are never used on websites. TIFs are almost always CMYK or greyscale (though they can be RGB for some applications such as digital textile printing).

EPS: use them in print

An EPS file is usually a high-resolution photo, or a vector file (an image, such as a logo, which is scalable to any size without loss of quality). EPS files can be CMYK or have Pantone colours.

HEIF/HEIC: a high-quality image format

The tech company Apple developed the 'high efficiency image format/container' (HEIF/HEIC) in 2017 to compress high-quality images captured on Apple devices. This new format can capture both video and audio (think Live Photos) and uses less of your device's storage than the same quality resolution images saved in JPEG format. Being so new, HEIC images currently have compatibility issues when transferred to non-Apple devices, but most convert to JPEG where needed.

DOC: usually a Microsoft Word file

A DOC file indicates it has been created in Microsoft Word. Some versions of Microsoft Word save the files as .docx. This just means it was made on a newer version of Microsoft Word.

RTF: a text file that can be opened on most devices

If you're not sure whether someone you're sending a .doc file to has Microsoft Word installed, a simple way to ensure they can open it is to save the file as .rtf. This stands for Rich Text Format, and just means the file can be opened in any number of other text-reading computer programs.

ZIP: a method to compress large files

Sometimes if you email someone a really big image or several images (totalling around 5 megabytes—5mb—or more), their email can reject it, or the email might never arrive. Disaster! However, if you ZIP a folder containing text or image files, that folder is compressed resulting in a smaller overall file size. Sometimes zipping images reduces the file size by a lot, sometimes only a little (there are dull technical reasons for this). If in doubt, email images separately or use an online file transfer system.

RAR: a method to compress large files

RAR files are essentially the same as ZIP files—a compressed file format small enough to send over email.

Other common file types you might encounter

FILE EXTENSION	PROGRAM
.ai	Adobe Illustrator
.psd	Adobe Photoshop
.indd	Adobe InDesign
.pptx	Microsoft PowerPoint
.xlsx	Microsoft Excel

How to distinguish a high-resolution file from a low-resolution one

There is a big difference between low-resolution and high-resolution images, and submitting the wrong file types to printers, publication editors, bloggers, online platforms, and your graphic or web designer can cause all sorts of headaches.

Why do you need high- and low-resolution versions of the same image?

It's always a good idea to have both high-resolution and low-resolution versions of all your marketing photographs saved somewhere for easy access. This should cover you for myriad marketing opportunities online and off, even at short notice. Ensure when you take photographs—or have them taken professionally by a photographer—the end result is images in high resolution. Low resolution images can be made from high-resolution images, but not the other way around.

Online platforms will generally specify image submission requirements, relating to size or image file type. If you are emailing your imagery to a human person, be mindful of the image size. Some email programs automatically reduce the file size (and therefore quality) of a high-resolution image when it is sent as an attachment.

To avoid this, send low-resolution images as JPEGs attached to the email, with a URL 'to the cloud' where high-resolution versions can be accessed.

Avoid putting images into a Word document or sending as a PDF. Attaching JPEGs to an email is the quickest way to have your imagery reviewed, or used as a placeholder. If the receiver needs a higher resolution file, they can access your cloud-stored versions, or request the high-resolution versions from you.

File transfer platforms and programs: an alternative to sending files via email

When email rejects an attachment because of its size or type, a file transfer system can be a safe alternative. Dropbox, WeTransfer, or Google Drive are just a few popular file transfer software platforms that are either free or have a free user option.

Any platform with 'Cloud' or 'Drive' in the name usually has a 'share' function (iCloud, Google Drive, OneDrive). Sharing a file means generating a unique URL link and sending it to someone. That person can then access the file via their internet browser and download it directly. It (usually) means they have permission to access only that file or folder, not everything else within your cloud storage.

Now when your designer asks if you can 'Dropbox' them a file or folder of files, you know it's about sharing a link via a file-sharing platform, not performing an interpretive dance move.

Determining image resolution

By file size

There are two really easy ways to determine the resolution of an image, so you can be sure to always supply an image that won't be so large it crashes the recipient's inbox, or be rejected by the recipient for being too small for its intended use.

The easiest way to check whether an image is high-resolution or low-resolution at a glance is to look at the file size details on your computer. For example, JPEG images above 1500KB are an indication of a high-resolution image (1000 kilobytes = roughly 1 megabyte). You can tell that an image is low-resolution if its size is a few hundred kilobytes or fewer.

If you're looking at the Details view of a folder of files on Windows, or you right click the image and select Properties, you can see the size of the image in kilobytes (KB).

On a Mac, you can select the file in Finder and see its infomation, or you can click More Info.

By pixel dimensions

Looking at the pixel dimensions of an image is also a good way to determine image resolution. Pixel dimensions give you the width and height of an image. It's as simple as more pixels = bigger image.

As a guide, 100x100 pixels translates to 1x1cm printed at 300DPI, so, 1000x1000 pixels will translate to an image that can be printed at a maximum of 10x10cm in high-resolution.

In your Details view on Windows, you can view a column called Dimensions—this will give you a measurement in pixels.

On a Mac, you can select the file in Finder and see its pixel dimensions, or you can click More Info.

High-resolution

Low-resolution

19

Paper and envelope sizes

The ISO (or International Organisation for Standardisation—doesn't that sound like a dream place to work for the more pedantic creative?) has a standard for paper sizes.

The A series

The ISO standard for paper is called the A Series. Each size in the A series is defined by halving the preceding paper size along the longest edge. A0 is the largest standard paper size in this group, and A7 is commonly the smallest.

The most common paper size, the one that fits inside your desktop printer for example, is A4. Double it and you have A3. Fold an A4 in half and you have A5, and so on.

The B series

The B-series is less commonly found than the A-series (in Australia at least), unless talking about book sizes or unusual brochure sizes. Sheet sizes for the B-series fall in-between sheet sizes of the A-series.

Envelopes: the C series

The ISO is at it again with their handy system of remembering which size of paper fits inside which envelope. Sure, calling it the 'E-series' would have made it easier to remember, but C is fine, I suppose. C-series envelopes complement A-series paper sizes.

US paper sizes

The commonly used paper sizes in the United States are based on the imperial system of measurement. 'Letter' is about equivalent to A4 in metric terms, and you'll likely recognise it by the default settings on your inkjet printer or software programs. (Fun fact: along with the USA, Liberia and Myanmar are the only other countries that use imperial measurement. So if you choose to use this system of measurement, they'll know what you're talking about in only three countries on Earth.)

What's the deal with DL?

Throwing a spanner in the works is DL, which refers to an A4 piece of paper folded into three. Brochures are often specified as a 'DL' size, as are standard business envelopes (the ones boring mail like bills and bank statements come in), but the two are slightly different sizes. What's up with that, ISO?

Business card sizes

There's no standard for business card sizes and sometimes the offbeat-sized ones are the most effective. But when it comes to 'standards' for business-card printing providers, you'll find 55mm x 90mm quite common. This size is also 'wallet size'.

Flyers, brochures and booklets: common sizes

Flyers, also known as leaflets—those single or double-sided pieces of paper that you'll find in your letterbox— are usually a standard size such as A5, A6 or DL.

Brochures are like flyers but generally have more pages and are folded: for example, an A4 piece of paper folded in half makes an A5 brochure. An A4 piece of paper folded in thirds makes a DL brochure. An A5 piece of paper folded in half makes an A6 brochure.

Booklets are an extension of brochures but are usually longer again, and with more pages that need to be stapled or sewn together (a.k.a. saddle stiched—see page 53) or bound in another way.

Binding and spines

If your project involves multiple pages—for example a book, booklet or report—you'll come across terminology about binding. Saddle stitching is the norm for shorter documents, around 16 pages or less. Perfect-bound documents feature a flat spine—the kind where the title of the document might appear—when several saddle-stitched sections are affixed together and covered with the, ah, cover. Whether or not it is important that your document lay flat when open is often a consideration when specifying binding. More on pages 43 and 45.

A-SERIES	Sheet size: width x height
A0	841mm × 1189mm
A1	594mm × 841mm
A2	420mm × 594mm
A3	297mm × 420mm
A4	210mm × 297mm
A5	148mm × 210mm
A6	105mm × 148mm
A7	74mm × 105mm

DL paper size	99mm x 210mm
DL envelope size	110mm x 220mm

B-SERIES	Sheet size: width x height
B0	1000mm × 1414 mm
B1	707mm × 1000 mm
B2	500mm × 707 mm
B3	353mm × 500 mm
B4	250mm × 353 mm
B5	176mm × 250 mm
B6	125mm × 176 mm
B7	88mm × 125 mm

US PAPER SIZES	Sheet size: width x height
Half Letter	140 x 216 mm (5.5 x 8.5 in)
Letter	216 x 279 mm (8.5 x 11.0 in)
Legal	216 x 356 mm (8.5 x 14.0 in)
Junior Legal	127 x 203 mm (5.0 x 8.0 in)
Ledger/Tabloid	279 x 432 mm (11.0 x 17.0 in)

C-SERIES	The envelope size: width × height	The paper or document size it fits (flat)
C3	458mm × 324mm	A3
C4	324mm × 229mm	A4
C5	229mm × 162mm	A5
C6	162mm × 114mm	A6
C7	114mm × 81mm	A7

Facts about fonts

Font v typeface: what's the difference?

In the B.C. era (Before Computers), words were printed onto a page via the lining up of individual letters cut from small metal or wooden blocks. Text on a page was laboriously laid out by hand in reverse order—each letter lined up next to one another to form words and sentences. (Yes, fixing typos at the last minute was a real headache).

Back then, a typeface was the name given to a family of fonts that had similar individual characteristics (those that made up the 'look' of the font). The font was the exact size, weight and/or style of the typeface that needed to be picked out by your printer from their little metal block stash and laid out in the order specified by the designer.

typeface	Times New Roman
font style	**Times New Roman Bold**
font size	**Times New Roman Bold, size 13**

After computers overtook this old method of type placement, the design and printing process sped up about a million percent, and suddenly the 'font' was merely a drop-down-menu click away. This democratisation of design meant that we didn't need to necessarily specify which typeface and which font any longer, and thus the two terms became rather interchangeable. For the purpose of this section, I'll use 'font' instead of 'typeface' (purists, please don't @ me).

Where do you find a font?

Fonts can be found in your home and online. There are millions of fonts in the world. Some come pre-installed on your computer, some are available for free and some you can buy online from type foundries (companies that design and sell fonts). Try searching for 'fonts' online and you'll find many options.

A font usually has a family

Some fonts are singular and some are part of a family. A font family might include variations of a main 'regular' font, for example an italic (or slanted) version, bold (thicker) version or a light (thinner) version.

There are two broad categories of fonts

Typeface designs are generally divided into two broad categories: display and text.

Display font

Display fonts are all well and good when used for a heading, logo, or sign which consists only of a few words. But you wouldn't use a display font for the text in a book—it may be legible but would quickly give the reader a headache. Some examples of other sub-categories of display fonts are script fonts and hand-drawn fonts (see page 50).

Text font

A text font is what you would use for the main text in a book. It is designed specifically to guide the eye and make reading a document easier on the brain (see page 50).

You don't have to use them all at once

Generally, it's best not to use too many different fonts within one design, although using a variety of versions of a single font family (Helvetica regular, Helvetica italic and Helvetica bold etc) makes sense and can aid comprehension of the text.

The difference between serif and sans-serif typefaces

Serifs are the little 'feet' at the bottom of some fonts like Times New Roman and Georgia. When words are strung together, these serifs form a virtual line underneath each word and help the eye to move from one word to the next more easily.

Sans-serif fonts don't have those feet at the bottom of each letter, but that doesn't mean they can't be used for longer-format text. (But take a look at any published novel—I guarantee the font used for the text of the book will be a serif.) Examples of popular sans-serif fonts are Helvetica, Gotham, Century Gothic and Arial.

Serif (little feet!) → **hello**

Sans-Serif (no feet) → hello

PCs and Macs can only use certain types of fonts, most of the time...

A font that works on a Mac may not work on a PC, for various technical reasons. This may mean the font you already have installed or purchased is unusable if you're collaborating with a designer who uses a different computer platform, or if you are changing from Mac to PC or vice-versa, you might need to repurchase the correct font file format.

...but now there's opentype!

Having said that, many fonts are now being converted to or designed as Opentype format, so one font type will work on both Mac and PC computers. Opt for this version if you buy a new font, or look for the extension '.otf' if supplying a font to a third party.

Do you have a licence to use that font?

Almost all fonts come with a licence, and whether you found them online for free or purchased them through a foundry, ensure you check the licence does not restrict the font to 'personal use only' (birthday invitation = okay; business logo design = not okay). There may also be restrictions on how many computers you can load the font onto and how you can share them with third-parties such as design and print service providers.

Using photographs and illustrations in graphic design

The difference between graphic designers, illustrators and photographers

While one person can have many skills with which to pay the bills, generally the roles of graphic designer, illustrator and photographer are assigned to different people for each project. A graphic designer may be able to produce basic illustrations, but should be seen as more of a curator of images and other illustrative content within the design.

'Whoa now! My project just got a lot more expensive', I see you thinking. Well, maybe yes, maybe no. While illustrations and photographs might form an important part of your graphic design project, there are a few different ways to procure them.

Stock image libraries

What is stock imagery?

Also known as royalty-free imagery, stock imagery—photographs and illustrations—are really useful for clients who don't have the budget for custom images, or when a custom image is not required simply to illustrate a point.

Stock image libraries work like this: photographs and illustrations are made by any number of content creators around the world and submitted to the library. The image library makes those images available to any user around the world, simply by paying a one-off 'licence' fee. These fees are usually determined by the style and content of the image, the resolution options available, and the exclusivity rights that can be assigned to the image. You pay the licence fee, and the image is yours to use within the bounds of that licence.

Easy, right? Here's the catch: a single image could be used by dozens, hundreds or thousands of people at the same time—across print and digital mediums. That's how these image creators earn money via stock image platforms. Instead of being paid to create an image for a single customer for exclusive use, they receive a portion of every licence fee paid by multiple users for the same image. So be wary if a stock image or illustration becomes a central part of your business' branding—it could also be used within myriad other contexts and businesses (or even by a competitor).

Stock image licences

Like the licences for fonts (see page 27), stock images may also come with a licence. Whether you found them online for free or purchased them through a stock image website, ensure that the licence does not restrict your intended use (preferably, before you fall in love with it!). Occasionally a royalty-free image licence will stipulate 'for editorial use only' or put a cap on the number of times the image can be reproduced under a single licence fee. Some licences dictate that images cannot be used in conjunction with sensitive content, or may have territorial-use restrictions.

The good news is, most royalty-free image licences or Creative Commons licences allow you to edit the image to your liking—so if you want to change its colours, or create a new image by combining multiple images, you're free to do so (provided you've purchased the original image licence, of course!). Learn more about Creative Commons on page 30.

Image watermarks

Stock libraries will often allow a user to download a low-resolution version of their chosen image, albeit emblazoned with a watermark of the image library. This is helpful in the sense that it allows a designer to use the low-resolution 'placeholder' so you, the client, may see how the image/s will work in the layout design. Try before you buy, so to speak. Only once it is ready to be presented to the world as part of the final design, does a non-watermarked version need to be purchased.

Where to find stock/royalty-free imagery

There are stock-image libraries to suit any budget. iStockphoto, Getty Images, Dreamstime, and Stocksy offer both illustrations and photographs. Libraries that offer free images without the need for licensing payment or attribution include Unsplash and Pexels.

Creative Commons

Creative Commons is a licensing model 'designed to encourage free use of works without fear of copyright infringement'.[1] The scheme works in a similar way to royalty-free image licensing, however in lieu of payment, the licensing conditions may require you to adhere to special conditions. An example of these conditions could be that attribution is to be given to the image creator where the work is included, or that the image can only be used in a non-commercial context. If you come across an image or illustration with a Creative Commons licence, ensure you check the licence type before it is supplied to the designer for use in your project.

Hiring professionals to create imagery for your project

There are many reasons why your project may need the services of a professional photographer or illustrator:

Custom imagery

Everything from the specificity of your communication (e.g. I am a plumber named Yvette, and this is a photograph of me and my van); to the number of different images you need in the same illustrative style (e.g. there are 27 different yoga poses you can teach your dog, and my book needs a diagram for each one!).

Authentic photos connect people to your brand, and say a thousand (hopefully good!) words about you. Nothing is more authentic than real photos of your real face, your real workplace, your real team.

Avoid the cliché

Because stock imagery is trying to appeal to multiple potential buyers and be applicable in many different contexts, it can step into the world of cliché. Scenes and scenarios can play out over a series of images, often around a set of specific key words. Think 'young couple buying a home', 'university students studying for exams', 'harried mum trying to have it all'. You've seen these images around. While staged imagery with a very clear subtext has its place, it can be tiresome and assumes only a base level of intelligence from your audience.

Exclusivity

Perhaps the style of illustrations or photographs in your marketing material is essential to your branding. It wouldn't be desirable to have a competing business use the same imagery as you, would it? This is where commissioning custom imagery for your brand can help you be heard and seen amongst the noise and lights of our information-heavy daily lives. Using custom imagery is an opportunity to excite your potential audience with something that is new, unseen, and innovative. And while you're at it, you can negotiate with your photographer or illustrator a set of licensing terms that suits your usage needs completely.

PART TWO

Designer dictionary: more common terms explained

Adobe Illustrator

A computer program developed by Adobe that deals primarily with illustration creation. Builds and deals with images that are vector illustrations and text, but not huge amounts of text. For example, you might use Illustrator to design a business card, but not a very text-heavy document like a book or a newsletter.

Adobe InDesign

Another computer program from Adobe that deals primarily with the layout and arrangement of text and images on a page to prepare it for printing. Can be used to create everything from a business card through to a flyer, newsletter or a long-format book.

Adobe Photoshop

Adobe again, this program deals primarily with images that are photographs—editing; changing colours; disguising or changing elements of the photograph's subject; converting to a new colour profile such as RGB, Greyscale or CMYK.

Application

Another word for computer program e.g. 'The application I used to create the logo was Adobe Illustrator', and also for the format in which a design will be used e.g. 'There will be three applications of the logo: on our letterhead, the brochure and our signage'.

Back-end

A web-design term referring to the coding behind the user interface of a website, making it functional.

Bevelled corner PAGE 51

A 45-degree cut applied to the corners of a paper product to remove the sharp point.

Bleed PAGE 54

The extension of an image or colour beyond the document's trim marks. Ensures that when a printed product is cut to size, even if the cut does not line up to the crop marks exactly, you can hardly notice because the print will still continue all the way to the edge.

Booklets

Multi-page documents, shorter than a book but longer than a brochure. Common sizes include DL, A4, A5 & A6.

Brand

The combination of an overall visual and communication style across products, presentation and customer relationships that form the 'personality' of a business.

Brief

A set of instructions from a client to a designer, outlining their design requirements, objectives and desired outcomes.

Browser

An application you use to see web pages. Safari, Google Chrome and Firefox are all browsers.

C-fold PAGE 53

When a piece of paper is folded into three and one flap sits underneath the cover flap. DL brochures are commonly folded this way.

Celloglaze or 'cello'

A laminate applied to the paper after printing to give a smooth, hardwearing effect. Note that not all celloglazes are created equal: some coatings are not suitable for writing on and their application may also prevent the paper from being recycled.

Coated paper

Coated papers have an ingredient added during the paper-making process that makes it smoother, less absorbent, and can make colours display with a slightly brighter effect than on uncoated paper.

Collateral PAGE 49

A collection of physical (and/or digital) elements created for a single brand, e.g. a brochure, postcard and advertisement might be referred to as marketing collateral for a new business launch.

Concept

An idea for a design, or the reasoning or message behind the design.

Content

The words or images within a document. You might be asked to 'provide content' which means you need to supply the words and/or images to the designer so they can make you a pretty document.

Copyright

I'm going to go with a proper dictionary definition here: 'A legal right, existing in many countries, that grants the creator of an original work exclusive rights to determine whether, and under what conditions, this original work may be used by others.'[2] For your project, the copyright holder could be the designer, or you the client, while the 'other' may be the designer, or you, the client! Learn more on pages 78–80.

Corporate colours

A suite of colours used consistently across a business's brand collateral.

Deboss

The opposite of emboss, where elements of the design are indented into the page.

Deep etched

When a product image is on a completely white background, or the background is made transparent via editing in Photoshop.

Die cut

A printing effect where shapes are cut out of paper (revealing what is underneath) or a standard rectangular or square shape is modified in some way.

Dieline

A line on a print-ready file that is not printed but tells the printer what shape to make the die cut.

DPI

DPI stands for dots per inch. It's a printing term from ye olde times before computers were a major component of the design and printing process and refers to the resolution of the image. The more dots-per-inch, the higher the quality of detail in the printed image. 300DPI is the standard required resolution for images intended for print, while images at 72DPI will appear pixellated when printed but will look fine when viewed on-screen. Note: the measurement is dots per linear inch, not dots per square inch.

Draft

A version of a design provided to the client for feedback.

Drop shadow PAGE 51

An effect applied to an image to make it look like it is three-dimensional and casting a shadow on the page.

DL brochure

A brochure, usually consisting of six DL-size pages (99mm x 210mm). Commonly folded in a C-fold or Z-fold (see page 53).

Dummy text PAGE 56

Displayed in concept designs in place of real information, to show how text would look aesthetically in the final design. Designers often use sections of faux-Latin text, known colloquially as Lorem Ipsum, as dummy text.

Emboss

The opposite of deboss, where elements of the design are raised on the page.

Feathered edge PAGE 51

Where the edge of an image is soft and 'dissolves' into the page.

Finished art

The stage at which an item is designed with all supplied information included and the design concept's aesthetic applied, then prepared as a draft or for sign-off. 'Finished Artist' is also a job title within the design industry referring to someone who does not conceive of the look and feel of the design, but merely implements it across various applications.

Flat colours

Solid blocks of colour in text, shapes, or parts of logos that do not have any colour variation.

Flyers

Single or double-sided pieces of paper, also known as leaflets. Common sizes include DL, A4, A5 & A6.

Foil/foil stamp

When metallic foil is printed on a page. This stands out more than metallic Pantone ink though it can be more expensive to apply.

Format

This word can be used in a couple of contexts within the graphic design world. As a noun it's about the state in which something exists, e.g. 'What format is your existing brochure in—hard copy or digital?' As a verb it can refer to the setting out of text and images, e.g. 'I'll format the text to adhere to your style guide'.

Free pitching

A practice that graphic designers usually frown upon, where a client will ask a designer to create a concept or work based on their brief, but only pay the designer if they choose to use the concept or work. Basically, to a designer, this is doing a lot of work for potentially no pay.

Gatefold PAGE 53

A type of fold commonly used for brochures where the cover panel is split in two and folds outward from the centre.

Gloss paper

The printed paper has a shiny surface.

Icon set

A simple graphic or set of related graphics that indicate

concepts visually, such as the 'bed, bath, car' icons commonly associated with real estate descriptions.

Image

Mostly refers to any photograph or illustration.

Imposed pages

A printer or designer will impose pages of a long-form document or book before it is sent to print, so that when bound the sections read in the right order.

Included fonts

A term referring to sending the fonts used in a document to a third party so that the document reproduces exactly on screen or in print.

Index colour

A method of compressing an image that restricts the image's colour palette in order to save computer memory. An indexed image appears like a puzzle of pixellated colour blocks, without a smooth visual transition between similar colour tones.

KB

Abbreviation for Kilobyte, e.g. 150KB. The uppercase is important—kb (lowercase) refers to kilobits, which is the speed of transfer of information over a computer network.

Kerning PAGE 56

The amount of space between two letters in a typeface. Sometimes a combination of two letters in a word, set in a particular typeface, can look visually odd unless the kerning is adjusted manually.

Keyline

A solid line that is used to divide or border text or images.
Not to be confused with a tasty type of citrus-flavoured pie.

Landscape PAGE 52

Refers to the orientation of a rectangular piece of paper,
where the longer edge is horizontal and the shorter edge is
vertical. The opposite is called portrait.

Layout

The process or stage of designing an item based on the
concept or mood board. A layout may incorporate dummy
text or live text.

Leading PAGE 56

The amount of space between two lines of text in a paragraph.

Leaflets

Single or double-sided pieces of paper, also known as flyers.
Common sizes include DL, A4, A5 & A6.

Licence

Permission to use a piece of creative work created by a third
party (such as an image, font or a finished design) for an
agreed purpose, and sometimes for a set amount of time.

Live text

Text in a document that is not outlined and thus can be
edited and changed.

Logo PAGE 48

A symbol which is connected to a brand or business to
distinguish itself from competitors.

Logotype PAGE 48

A corporate mark where the typeface of the brand name becomes recognisable as its logo.

Look and feel

A term referring to how a brand represents itself to its customers—e.g. certain fonts, colours, and graphics.

Margin/Safe margin PAGE 56

The blank space that borders content on a page. A 'safe margin' is the space between the content of a page and the edge of a page which may be cut off during the printing process.

Mark/Corporate mark

A fancier word for logo.

Matte paper

Printed paper which is not shiny.

MB

Abbreviation for Megabyte, e.g. 5MB.

Mock-up

A model of a design or product, or prototype, usually used when referring to stationery or other printed items, and how the item will look when professionally printed or produced.

Mood board

A collection of visual references to describe a designer's concept.

Outlined fonts

A term referring to a precautionary measure taken by graphic designers to ensure text in a document reproduces exactly when sent to a third party e.g. a printer.

Paragraph space PAGE 56

The amount of space between two paragraphs.

Perfect bound

Refers to the binding of a document, where the pages and cover are glued together at the spine. This method has a square spine and a book with a very low number of pages can't be perfect bound.

Perforation

Those little dots that make a page easy to tear off.

Pixel

A tiny dot on your computer screen—they group together in different colours to form everything you see on screen.

Pixellated PAGE 19

A term referring to the obvious low-resolution of an image, where the individual pixels that make up the image are clearly visible and the crispness of the image is lost. Commonly occurs when an image is enlarged past the point of appropriate resolution for its size.

Plates

A printing term that refers to the actual physical hardware required to print your document. One plate is required for each colour in each and every printed document. CMYK printing requires four plates: Cyan, Magenta, Yellow and Black. A two-colour print job would require two plates for both Pantone colours specified.

Point

A term of measurement to determine the size of a font or the thickness of a keyline or stroke.

Pop

A colloquial term for making a statement or standing out amongst other nearby items. Often used to refer to colour treatment in a design, e.g. a bright or bold Pantone ink, when used sparingly against more muted elements, might make a design feature really 'pop'.

Portrait PAGE 52

Refers to the orientation of a rectangular piece of paper, where the shorter edge is horizontal and the longer edge is vertical. The opposite is called landscape.

Print-ready file

The term given to a design file that is finished and ready to be sent to the printer. If it's to be printed on paper, the print-ready file will most likely have all fonts outlined or included, all images converted to CMYK, with bleed, and printer's marks indicated on the file. However, it's important to talk to your printer about your specific project to gauge their requirements for a print-ready file, as printers and processes vary greatly.

Printer's marks PAGE 54

A collective term for trim marks, fold marks, bleed marks, registration marks and colour bars. All the stuff outside of the design file that tells the printer how to make a flat, blank piece of paper into the finished product you require.

Proof

A printed or digital sample of finished design work provided for sign off.

Quote

An estimate of the time and cost a design job will take to complete, provided to the client on receipt of a brief.

Raster image

An image created with pixels that are not scalable to any size without loss of quality. Photographs (images made up of billions of colours) are raster images.

Registration marks PAGE 54

Marks to assist a printer to align inks (colours) on a page before printing. Mis-alignment is referred to as 'mis-registration'.

Resolution PAGE 19

The detail of an image made up of pixels. Therefore: low-resolution = not much detail; high resolution = lots of detail.

Reverse brief

A document provided by the designer to the client, clarifying the client's design requirements, objectives and desired outcomes. Often a reverse brief also includes an interpretation of the deliverable elements and timeframes so that the designer can ascertain they are on the 'same page' with the client before beginning the design work.

Round corners PAGE 51

An effect applied to the corners of a paper product to remove the sharp point. The most common radius is around 5mm.

Saddle stitched

Refers to the binding of a document, usually with two staples or stitches along the spine. When you open the document to the centre pages you can see the staples or stitches. Using this method of binding, you can't print anything on the spine of the book/booklet.

Sign off

Approval from a client before a major part of a project goes ahead (usually one that requires a sum of money to be paid by the client, either to the designer or a third party). Things such as printing, a website going live, or commencing production often require 'sign off' from the client, assuring the designer that all information is correct and everything looks as it should.

Specifications (specs)

The details of a graphic design job, commonly referring to size, number of colours, and quantity (if printed).

Spot gloss/spot varnish

A transparent glossy/shiny ink printed onto paper as a feature element.

Stock image

A royalty-free illustration or photograph usually purchased from an online library for a fee. Stock images are usually not exclusively licensed to any one user.

Stroke

Another term for keyline.

Style guide

A document which prescribes how a business should present itself visually to a customer via its use of logo, fonts, colour and imagery across all publicly-visible mediums (such as stationery, signage, brand collateral etc).

Swing tag

A tag that is attached to an item of clothing or product in a store, which shows the brand name, and often sizing and price details. Not to be confused with a care label which describes the washing instructions of an item of clothing.

Template

Usually refers to a design file that you can edit or produce different versions from as needed, e.g. a newsletter design template.

Tint

A slightly lighter version of a solid colour. Tints can be 1–99% of a solid colour. Particularly useful if you're limited to using one or two Pantone colours and want some variety of tones.

Transparent

See-through or clear.

Trim marks/crop marks PAGE 54

Indicators on a print-ready file that tell the printer where to cut and what size the finished item should be.

Trim size

The size of the paper or printed product when it is finished.

Uncoated paper

The paper is more absorbent and has a more textured feel, and colours reproduce with a slightly duller effect than on coated paper.

Vector image

An image created with pixels that are scalable to any size without loss of quality. Logos, text and other images that feature only a few colours are most often vector images.

Z-fold PAGE 53

When a piece of paper is folded into three, concertina-style.

COMPANY

Logo

COMPANY®

Logotype

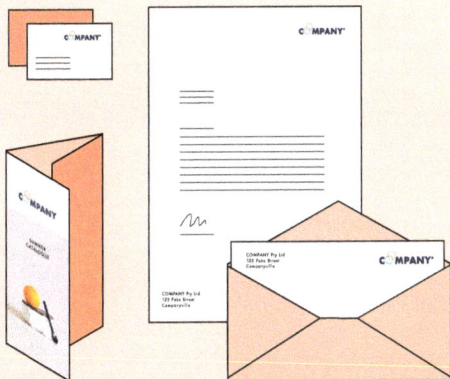

Collateral

Serif

Sans-serif

DISPLAY

Hand-drawn

Script

Bevelled corners

Feathered edge

Drop shadow

Round corners

51

Portrait orientation

Landscape orientation

Saddle stitched

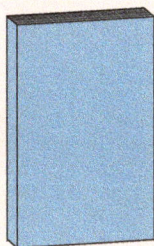

Perfect bound

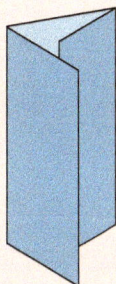

C-fold

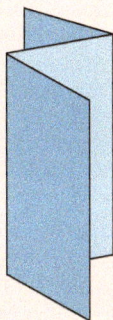

Z-fold

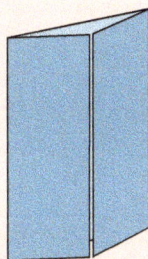

Gatefold

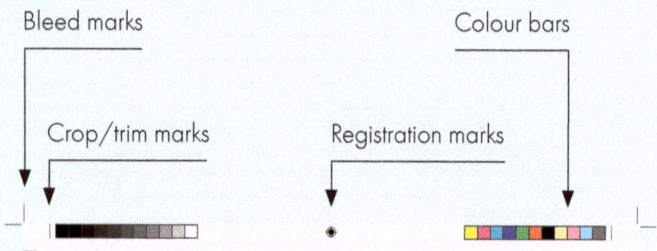

The heading

THE SUBTITLE

Lorem ipsum dolor sit amet, conse
tetur adipiscing elit, sed do eiusmod
tempor incididunt ut labore et dola.

Sed ut perspiciatis unde
omnisbelle iste natus error
sit voluptea atem accusan
tium dol remque laudan tium,
totamora el allsa rem aperi am,
eaque ipsa quae ab illo inventore
veritatis et quasi archi tecto
beatae vitae dict sunt explicabo.

Nemo enim ipsam voluptatem
quia voluptas sit aspernatur aut
odit aut al oro fugit, sed quia
consequuntur magni dolores eos
qui ratione volupt atem sequi
nesciunt. Neque porro quisquam
est, qui ora dolorem ipsum quia
dolor sit amet, consectetur.

Printer's marks

Bleed area (will be cut off)

Safe margin (may be cut off)

Margin (space around text area)

The heading

THE SUBTITLE

Lorem ipsum dolor sit amet, conse
tetur adipiscing elit, sed do eiusmod
tempor incididunt ut labore et dola.

S ed ut perspiciatis unde
omnisbelle iste natus error
sit voluptea atem accusan
tium dol remque laudan tium,
totamora el ailsa rem aperi am,
eaque ipsa quae ab illo inventore
veritatis et quasi archi tecto
beatae vitae dict sunt explicabo.

Nemo enim ipsam voluptatem
quia voluptas sit aspernatur aut
odit aut al oro fugit, sed quia
consequuntur magni dolores eos
qui ratione volupt atem sequi
nesciunt. Neque porro quisquam
est, qui ora dolorem ipsum quia
dolor sit amet, consectetur.

Margins and bleed

Kerning

Lorem Ipsum (dummy text)

The head

THE SUBTITL

Leading

Lorem ipsum dolor sit ar
adipiscing elit, sed do eiu
incididunt ut labore et do

Drop cap

Sed ut perspiciatis unde omnis iste natus error sit volupt atem accusan tium dol remque laudan tium, totamora el a rem aperi am, eaque ipsa quae ab illo inventore veritatis et quasi archi tecto beatae vitae dicta sunt explicabo.

Paragraph space

Nemo enim ipsam voluptatem quia voluptas sit aspernatur aut odit aut al oro fugit, sed quia consequuntur magni dolores eos qui ratione volupt atem sequi nesciunt. Neque porro quisquam

est, qu
sit am
velit, :
eius m
labore
aliquar
enim a
nostru
corpori
nisi u
conseq
eum iu
volupt;
molest
qui dol

Margin   Justified paragraph   Gutter

Greyscale

Bitmap

Gradient

Halftone

PART THREE

Building something great together

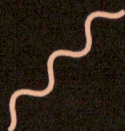

If you think
good design
is expensive,
you should
see the cost
of bad design.

RALF SPETH

Working with a professional graphic designer

Why and when it's a good idea

Whatever it is that you do for a living, I bet you do it pretty well. You might have studied to learn everything about your field, you might have worked really hard for years accumulating a specific skill set and a tonne of knowledge. Professional graphic designers have done that as well! Not only are they trained in the technical tools of graphic design, they were likely called to the profession because of a deep-seated or inate skill set that involves acute perception of colour, light, space, shape and line, mixed with a strategic business acumen focused on communication and messaging. It's a big ol' soup that takes a certain person to deliver a splendid result, that—to be quite honest—gives people an indescribably pleasant feeling when they interact with it.

Here is a short list of things that graphic designers know that you (if you DIYd) might not:

How to...

- space text so it doesn't give readers an actual headache
- choose colours that work best for the intended audience or mood of the design
- harness the power of space, and the particular combination of lines, shapes and colours, to engage the viewer

- ensure your brand colours are a similar hue across all its online and offline applications, to strengthen your brand identity and make it more recognisable to your customers
- apply a simple, creative idea across multiple applications—large and small, offline and online, from a business card to a company car
- make your not-so-great but necessary photos look great
- create a concept that can adapt to multiple formats, from billboards to book covers, posters to podcast artwork
- ensure you're using photos, fonts and other third-party stuff that you're actually allowed to use
- objectively present your business to the world in the best possible light

Which is not to say you don't or couldn't learn to do the things on this list. But really, don't you have other important business-sustaining things to focus on, that only you can do? Outsource the design to the experts—it's too important an investment in your success not to.

A short menu of graphic design professionals

One of the things I learned early on about the graphic design industry is that 'everyone needs a graphic designer'. And luckily, given the relatively low cost of the basic tools and digital assets one needs to 'set up shop' as a professional in the industry, there's a graphic designer for everyone's budget out there. This means it's highly likely you can engage a professional not only to suit your business's needs, but also your budget.

Freelancers/solopreneurs

From those who work on the occasional freelance gig after hours, to 'companies of one' working standard office hours, finding this kind of designer should be as easy as asking for recommendations from friends and professional contacts.

Things to consider

Freelance graphic designers are often willing and able to take on jobs that have smaller budgets (their generally low overheads mean they don't require a minimum spend) or require a shorter investment of time.

With a freelancer, you're working WITH the creative doing the work—not communicating through an account manager or other third party. This can make the creative process more collaborative, agile, and faster.

Finding the right fit

Understand, not all freelancers are created equal. Freelancers choose this business model for a variety of reasons, and it's worth attempting to determine when and how they work to ensure they are a good fit for your expectations. Do they work full-time or part-time hours? Are those hours daylight or nocturnal (it's quite possible the freelance life works for them because they're a night owl!). Is this something they do while balancing other work or family care? Are they nomadic travellers, working 'on the road'? What is their availability to complete your project within your timeline?

Whatever their reason for working the hours that they do, ultimately the project timeline is the anchor. Be sure to communicate early and often your timelines, hopes and dreams for the project—so those who are balancing multiple projects, working on the road, or operating outside of traditional business hours, can be sure to meet them.

Timelines and communication

Some solo operators might work from home; others in co-working spaces or shared offices. Meetings might not happen 'at their studio'—a coffee shop is often the freelancer's best friend, and they might not entertain the idea of sitting with you as you work if their work space is also their home.

Also be aware of how you wish to communicate with your designer. Do you need to meet in person first, or at various intervals throughout the job? Is an email-only relationship okay? Some freelancers prefer the 'working alone at home' model because it reduces the amount of in-person contact they wish to have each day (no judgement).

When undertaken tactfully, a conversation about timelines and communication expectations can reduce your risk of disappointment or feeling left in the dark, awaiting an update. And also note, working with a designer is a two-way street—they might very well ask the same questions of you before taking on your project.

Design studios

Graphic design studios can range in size from two people to 50 or more, but according to the Australian Graphic Design Association, most range from four to ten employees. Within this business there would typically be a few graphic designers, an account manager or two, a studio manager/traffic controller (yep, actual title), admin support, and a creative director or founder at the helm. Specialists with expertise in branding, digital/user-experience (UX) design, and app design may also be on staff, or contracted as projects require. Generally, design studios are multidisciplinary, but some specialise primarily in branding, packaging or digital design.

Things to consider

Due to higher overheads (all those pay packets, multiple tables and chairs, computers for everyone, teabags in the kitchen), the projects they take on may have higher budget thresholds, and their project fees may be greater.

You may have contact with the creative or creatives who are working on your project, but you may also only have contact with the company founder, creative director or account manager. And in the day and age of remote working, it's possible they're not all in the same building/city/country at the same time.

But this is not necessarily a bad thing. We can't all be good at everything, and having dedicated staff look after various aspects of your project—from creative, to production, to overall project management of the myriad third-party providers might be required to bring your project baby to life.

Design studios are often multidisciplinary or 'full service', meaning they are able to take care of multiple parts of a project that a freelancer or solo graphic designer might not be willing to take on. Think: the copywriting for your custom-built website; the printing and proofreading of your book; the beta testing of your app. If you want an all-in-one approach instead of project-managing multiple freelancers yourself, a design studio is worth the investment.

Other businesses offering 'graphic design'

When I said before that the barrier to entry for graphic design is low, I wasn't kidding. Without an accreditation system in place, take a computer and a couple of free or low-cost apps and you could technically start a graphic design business. Businesses who specialise in printing, IT or digital design may offer graphic design services. And depending on your needs, they might suffice.

Things to consider

This is where you really might need to consider the specialists vs generalists approach. If graphic design is tacked on the end of a list of services, is it their priority? What's important in your project—that it exists, or that it exists and communicates effectively to its desired audience?

Many brochures exist, printed in numerous quantities by very high-quality machines. But does the message they seek to convey grab and hold the attention of its recipient? That's a graphic designer's primary task. Not an afterthought.

Having said that, as with design agencies, many businesses expand their workforce per project and contract specialists to assist with specific client needs. If the one-stop-shop idea appeals to you, just ensure your expectation of effective design matches what the business can offer.

Specialists v generalists

So, you've had a logo designed. Good for you! Now, what do you want to do with it? Put it on a business card to give to people you meet? Display it at the top of a website? Stick it to your car? All valid platforms. But be aware, the highly talented person who designed that very good looking logo may not be able to design that business card, or build that website, or print and affix it to your car. Perhaps they are a specialist. But perhaps you don't want to go from shop to shop gathering all the bits you need. Perhaps you need: a generalist.

Things to consider

When looking to engage a graphic designer, it helps to be prepared. Prepared with a list of things that you think, or know, will form 'the meat on the bones'. For example, a range of stationery featuring the logo that is to be designed. A website and the words and images on it. A book and the illustrations inside.

Some graphic designers have broad skills—they can design a logo, build a website, take photos and maybe even write copy. But some are specialists, and they like to keep it that way. Ideally it will be fairly obvious where a specialist's strengths lie from their portfolio of work: you might even engage them based on their distinct and unique skill base.

All you need to know is, it helps to communicate your project needs and ascertain early on if you can (or even want) one person or studio to be with you from start to finish. If you're expecting that your book designer can then build the website to sell the book, it pays to ask up front.

Where to find a graphic designer

When you've decided the type of design service provider you need, it's time to find someone who fits the bill. But where to look? Some avenues to stroll down are noted below. Take your time with this part of the process: you'll make up time later when the work the designer produces is to your taste and the personality cocktail is mixed just right.

The personal recommendation

Ideally, you'll want someone whose work you feel a connection to, and if they come personally recommended, all the better. You're about to engage in a (somewhat) long-term relationship. This is where it pays to be set up on a 'blind date' with a designer thanks to a trusted friend or colleague. Temperament, expectations, and outcome can be canvassed with someone you trust or respect before making contact. But remember, everyone has different project goals, design styles and personality traits—someone who clicked and did great work for someone you know, might not be the best person to engage for your project.

The savvy social media marketer

It's a web within the web: these days you can find out anything via a quick hashtag or search on your favourite social media platform. Many design studios and freelance designers use social platforms to extend their website portfolios and offer deeper insight into both the range of design work they engage in, and their personality. Try hashtags that relate to your location and follow designers whose work you like to get a sense of how they operate as a person and a business. Of course, these feeds are usually highly curated and may feature work that 'inspires' the designer, rather than work they have actually created. Use a critical eye.

The top hit on Google

Google's a strange beast—you can pay your way to page 1, or you can earn your right to be there. Depending on the specifics of your search, Google may bring up the goods. Like the savvy social marketer, you'll learn more about their ethos, personality, and style through a little website research (plus additional Googling).

Guilds, associations, and professional groups

Professional groups can be a great place to search for a designer because, for a start, you know they must be somewhat professional if they belong to an association. Designers who pay an annual fee to be a part of these collectives usually do so because they are supporters of the group's ethos or mission (which often aims to extend credibility and professionalism in the marketplace, and offers professional development opportunities to its members). What this means for you, as a client, is often an aggregated list of professional designers who are ready to take your call.

GOOD

FAST

CHEAP

PICK TWO

How much will it cost?

An initial enquiry as to how much a graphic designer charges per hour, or an over-the-phone request for a 'ballpark figure', is not a great way to ascertain what it will cost for a designer to complete your project. We're detail-oriented folks: we love, nay, need details. This includes providing enough information so we can give you an accurate quote.

Requesting a quote: what you should provide

Some information about yourself and your goals

Like it or not, this is a relationship. It's transactional, but not in a 30-seconds-at-the-counter, brief-comment-about-the-weather kind of way. Your designer wants to help you achieve your business goals and look good doing it. So be honest, be vulnerable. There's no need to go into too much detail, but if you sell your project and give the designer an understanding of what you hope to achieve, it will help set the tone for the project and give the designer a better understanding of how clear YOU are about the outcome you desire.

A complete list of things you want designed

Remember on page 69 when we talked about the meat and the bones? You may not yet have thought of everything you want designed, but you probably have a pretty good idea. Make a list. If you think some things might not actually make it to fruition, group them and ask your designer to provide an itemised quote.

Without this list at the beginning of a project, you could find yourself in the land of scope-creep (see page 83). No-one wants that.

Your budget

Look, we get it. The cat and mouse game... don't reveal your budget in case the designer was thinking of charging a lot less and you get what you want for a steal. But when all is said and done, for a professional, it helps to reveal your cost expectations up front.

Receiving a quote: what to expect

The thing about most graphic design work is that it's bespoke. Just for you. Every idea, every computer mouse click, every choice the designer you've approached has made from their very unique and talented brain. Thus, every quote is bespoke.

Graphic designers often pursue one of these pricing strategies when quoting on a project.

Hourly rate

One designer's hourly rate may differ from another's, and when you really think about it, it's like comparing apples and oranges. If Designer A charges $50 an hour but takes six hours to make the requested changes to your brochure, and Designer B charges $150 an hour and takes one hour to make the same changes—which one is a better investment? Skills, efficiency, aptitude, and service are all variable.

The downside to agreeing to pay a designer an hourly rate might be the same as asking 'how long is a piece of string'? This is where a conversation about your budget is an important starting point. If a designer has set their hourly rate, they are unlikely to deviate. And it's quite possible that your expectations of 'how long something should take' is quite different from the reality.

Flat fee

Generally, a flat fee for a job is the best option for all involved. A designer will likely estimate the number of hours a similar job has taken to complete, multiplied by their hourly rate (a rate that is commensurate with their experience and expertise), and adding or subtracting additional extras that are contained in your brief. Allowances for a few rounds of changes are generally included, as are things like the designer's taxes, electricity, retirement saving, rent, water, doors, walls and the very computer they are working on. The good thing about this kind of quote is that everything that is included—and conversely, things that are not included—are right there on paper. So you're able to see what you're paying for and have a way to budget your project from the outset.

Value-based pricing

The value of a piece of graphic design work is both subjective and 100% worth taking into consideration when quoting a job. The present-day value of the Nike 'swoosh', a logo created by an American design student, is around 26 billion dollars. To design it, Carolyn Davidson was paid around $45.00. In some cases—and it could be the case with your project—the design is what is going to 'sell' whatever it is you're selling. Thus, not only does due process need to be given in its creation, but the value of that design work to your business might be understandably inflated.

No arguing, no ghosting

If you've received a quote from a designer, and have to 'pick yourself up off the floor', then I gather it's more than you expected it would cost. Based on what? If you're surprised a logo could cost you more than your weekly pay packet, then think about this: your weekly pay packet doesn't include what your employer has paid—on your behalf—for the place in which you work and everything inside it. We have business expenses too—that fee isn't simply money for jam.

Design is a commodity, but it is also your prerogative to shop around.

If it turns out that the cost estimates for the project are beyond what you had (secretly) budgeted or even imagined, then say so. Nothing feels worse than starting a relationship with someone (and getting to know them, even just enough to quote on a project), only to have them disappear once the quote comes through.

It's okay to negotiate

If a designer sends you a quote and the fee is more than you expected, it's okay to be honest about this. Ask if there is any elements that can be negotiated. But be real: this is unlikely to result in a lower price for the same amount of work. You'll have to be okay with a trimmed version of the scope of work. Maybe there's only two options instead of three. Maybe there's no included rounds of changes, and you'll simply pay for what you use. If your quote is bespoke, change is possible.

Commencement invoices, deposits, and kill fees

It's not uncommon that upon your approval of a designer's quote, they may invoice you for a deposit upfront (which will most likely be a percentage of the total quoted amount, and may or may not be refundable). Jobs with a low total fee may require full payment upfront.

A 'kill fee' or termination fee may also be set in a designer's terms and conditions, in the event that along the way you decide to not follow through with your project to its final stage. Remember, even though you might no longer have a need for the final product, the designer has likely still spent time and effort on your project and expects fees accrued so far will be paid by you, the client.

Copyright and contracts

Why have a contract?

You may have heard the saying: when you assume, you make an 'ass' out of 'u' and 'me'. However groan-worthy, the message is clear. Assume nothing. Inquire, question, and get everything in writing. While it won't go the whole way in protecting you from invoice surprises or being told no when you assumed 'the customer is always right', it will put the designer's needs and your rights and responsibilities in black and white.

Terms and conditions, agreements, and proposals

Be wary of designers who don't offer some form of terms and conditions or an agreement alongside a quote for their services. What happens if they ghost you, or for whatever reason can't complete a project? What can you do or not do with their work once you've paid your invoice? What expectations do you have around the confidentiality of your project, and how do they respect those wishes? Who pays for mistakes, when the mistakes end up costing cold, hard cash? These are things that, if assumed by either party, can end up fracturing a relationship when the unexpected occurs.

A designer's contract may not be laden with 'sign-here' stickies, but if it is presented and perceived to have been read and accepted, then it is legally binding.[3]

Copyright

Who owns copyright in a design?

Who owns copyright in the final work—or indeed, any individual bits or part of the final work that have been created during the process—is unique to every project. Ideally, a graphic designer will have a clause in their terms and conditions or contract about copyright ownership, and a discussion about it should have taken place before work began.

The upshot is, if a designer created something for you— a logo, a brochure, a layout—something where they chose the typefaces and the colours, placed images where they thought they should rightly go and pressed the buttons on the computer to make it happen, then they own the copyright to that something.

Now, it doesn't mean they own your business name, or a photo you took, or the words you wrote. In fact it might be that they just own a very small part of the project—the bit they created. Yep, it can be a complex concept for everyone to get their heads around, and while it might be easier to ignore the whole issue all together, it's smarter to face it head on and be clear on the issue of copyright.

Note that individual elements that neither you nor the designer created for your projects—such as photographs, illustrations and typefaces may be subject to their own copyright licenses. (See pages 28–32).

Licensing a design vs purchasing copyright outright

There's a tacit agreement that if you engage a graphic designer to create something specifically for you, you have a licence to use it for the purposes for which it was created. Own a burger restaurant and need a logo for your signage, packaging, and social media avatar? You can use the logo for those things, if that's what was agreed upon with the designer initially. But imagine for a second that your Burger Biz's popularity exceeds your expectations. Yay! And you open multiple outlets each sporting their own 'spin' on the original logo design (and your cousin, who has since become pretty good with Photoshop, makes the design edits). And/or the custom-designed burger-character, a key part of the logo, is so beloved by your customers that it is used to sell t-shirts bearing its likeness at a sweet profit for the business. What then? Well, things with copyright ownership can get murky, and your original designer may have grounds for a copyright infringement claim.

Think of a book cover. A cover that, thanks to your graphic designer, is so eye-catching and so recognisable that the book is a bestseller, and is on-sold to publishers who produce new editions in 20 different languages, the covers of which are based on the original design. Your designer will likely be unhappy that their intellectual property—purchased by you for a fee for that original book—is now being piggybacked for profit by myriad third-parties.

Or in a more common scenario: your newest competitor, who is quickly building an audience and potentially siphoning business from your established brand, has a logo eerily similar to, and often mistaken for, your business. Who can take legal action? Not you, or at least not as easily, if you don't own the copyright in the logo design. Ouch.

The solution? Have a conversation up front with your graphic designer about copyright. Be clear on the terms. If it costs you a little more to purchase outright copyright in the final design, then chalk this up to the price of freedom and security. But if an implied licence to use the logo, with rights to change or enhance the licence at a time that you see fit, works for you? Propose it, and a good graphic designer will be happy to be clear on the terms as well.

How to save yourself dollars and headaches (good practice for clients)

Communication

Graphic design can be otherwise thought of as communication design—so communication is a pretty important part of the process.

Ideally, when you first engage a designer, you have had some sort of communication about communication—that is, about whether you prefer to keep in touch throughout the duration of a project via email, on the phone, videoconferencing, in person, text, apps/web platforms, or any combination of those things.

Giving feedback

The best designers will be upfront about how they present drafts, concepts and iterations of the project to you for feedback, and how they would like that feedback to be presented back to them. For example, a feedback portal might link in with their project management systems. Some prefer feedback to be in writing so it can be referred back to (if feedback is provided over the phone or in person, an 'in writing' version might follow to confirm what it is that needs to be revised.)

Whatever method is used to provide your designer with comment or critique, the best type of communication is constructive, informative and... how to put this... frequent, but not too frequent. More 'contemplative yet decisive' and less 'stream of consciousness 4am thoughts'. No-one wants to wake up to a wall of new emails from the same sender. If you need to talk it out, pick up the phone, or request a phone call. The best designers will be happy to talk through your thoughts, allay concerns, and propose solutions.

If a detail changes

As mentioned earlier, designers are all about the details. What you might think is a small change might actually upset the foundation of a project—or it might just be a quick, easy fix. Regardless, letting the designer know about any kind of hiccup, adjustment or modification will help them continue to make the correct choices for the design process—and likely help avoid a hairline crack morphing into a chasm (or, you know, your phone number being printed incorrectly on a business card).

Cancelling, quitting, and putting projects on hold

Shit happens. To everyone, often when we least expect it. Sometimes the writing is on the wall, and sometimes it isn't. Regardless, fundamentally a relationship with a professional designer is like any other relationship: it's two human beings trying to achieve a goal together. If you need to cancel, quit, or put a project on hold, give the other human the respect of being upfront. Oftentimes a designer's contract or terms and conditions will allow for this kind of exit (sometimes called a kill fee), or terms can be negotiated to restart the project at a later date.

Be aware that if work has begun, you may be liable to pay the designer for the time they have already invested, regardless of whether or not the work will ultimately be used for its intended purpose. Chalk that money up to an investment gone bad, or a lesson learned. But don't ghost—you could find yourself in breach of contract.

Scope-creep

No, not the name of an indie rock band. Scope-creep is what designers call the unsubtle way in which an initial project scope slowly but surely (or sometimes, quite obviously and distinctly) gets larger and more complicated than initially described and/or quoted. Items that weren't in the initial project brief are added here and there, without a conversation about the extra time and resources being invested. If you have entered into an agreement that is some form of flat or project fee, this can be especially difficult for the designer and for your budget when a 'revised' invoice is presented at the end.

Be respectful of the designer's time and administrative tasks, and if you realise after the project commences that there are actually MORE things that you'd love a designer to help you with, ask for a revised quote (and don't be offended if a designer presents this to you either).

Timelines and schedules

A question most often posed to a client alongside 'what is your budget?' is: 'what is your timeline?'. Both speak to the viability of your desired outcome and the suitability of a particular designer to your project. It's not uncommon for a designer to be booked weeks or months in advance, nor is it uncommon for a designer to plot out and plan their project schedule based on the perceived timelines of a bunch of unrelated clients.

If you want your project prioritised, it helps to be upfront about your timeline (especially as it relates to upcoming launches, openings, deadlines etc). Remember that there are parts of the design-to-final-project process that can appear hidden—printing times, delivery times, waiting on third-party content. Take your designer's advice here: they deal with these providers daily. Some of them can be expedited, some cannot. The back-and-forth nature of feedback rounds can put the onus on you to adhere to a timeline, too. If project goals are clear from the outset, the best designers will do everything in their power to adhere to a timeline and make magic happen within the goalposts (just as long as they don't shift during the game).

Addressing big changes to a schedule or timeline

As noted earlier, sometimes things happen that can't be helped. People get sick, personal matters overtake business needs, people estimate a task will take less time than it actually does, etc etc. Sometimes unexpected opportunities pop up that put pressure on an already agreed-upon timeline. Here's where your well-tended relationship with your designer can help. Changes to schedules and timelines can be made, negotiations undertaken, and all-nighters can be pulled. The results can be varied (and in the case of all-nighters, sometimes costly!). Communicate, communicate, communicate.

Project complete!
What to ask for now
(and how to ask for it)

Your logo as various file types

A good designer will provide you with your final logo design in a variety of file types for present and future use, such as:

RASTER	
.jpeg, .jpg	high and low resolution for use online and in print
.gif, .png	with and without transparent elements, for digital applications
.tiff, .tif	very high-resolution raster files
VECTOR	
.eps .ai	can be scaled to any size (just in case you need it for a billboard or the side of a zeppelin)

Revisit page 13 to learn more about these file types.

You'll also want to ensure:

- All typefaces are outlined
- Colours have been converted to CMYK/RGB/Pantone as appropriate
- There are no embedded raster files within a vector file. (If there are, it could mean your logo can't be scaled indefinitely to any size).

Names of typefaces (and where to find them)

If you love the fonts your designer used in your logo/brochure/book/poster, that's awesome. Even more awesome is strengthening your brand or product recognition through consistent use of those typefaces and colours across other supporting elements of your business, like your website, business card, uniforms, signage, packaging and the like. So be sure to ask for the name of the typefaces or font family used in the design, and ideally, where to purchase a licence to use the font (by installing it on your computer and/or the computers of your employees).

Do you have a licence for that thing?

As mentioned on page 27, most typefaces require licences to use them. While there are many free fonts on the internet, some are only free for personal use (like on a birthday invitation, or passive-aggressive office kitchen sign). The best ones—designed professionally by a human as any usable product is—and those deemed for commercial use, cost money. It's usually a one-time payment, per user or per device install. That means, even if your designer has a licence, you'll need one too, especially if you use the font to create your own on-brand communication materials later on.

Colour breakdowns

Similar to typefaces, colour is hugely important in conveying a consistent brand message. But colour can be fickle. Go to a hardware store: how many different shades of blue are there? Your 'blue' can look different on screen, on paper, on a different kind of paper, on a sign, on your embroidered patch and on the car you just had sprayed. A good graphic designer will provide you with breakdowns—or codes—for the colours that make up your 'brand'. Flip back to Part One of this book, and have a read. Then you'll know that it's important to ask for the CMYK, RGB, Hex and Pantone colour names, to keep in your back pocket.

A style guide

All the info above? Typically it's the kind of thing collated and presented in a style guide. Branding style guides are common when you're a big corporate or NFP and are constantly slapping your logo on things (and want it to be slapped on in a consistent way). But really, any business big or small, or indeed any project, could warrant a style guide to ensure the presentation of a logo, supporting typefaces, colours, copywriting 'tone of voice', photography style, and more is kept consistent across any platform (or by anyone needing to implement it, anywhere). Consider asking your designer for a style guide on completion of your project. You may have to pay more for this added service, but if you're prone to the DIY approach and need a little hand-holding to keep things looking neat and tidy, it's a worthwhile investment.

Raw files

Graphic designers are individual when it comes to how they like to use and disclose their 'raw' files. By raw files, I mean the program files they created your work in: usually Adobe Illustrator, Photoshop, InDesign and the like. Their wariness to deliver these files to you may come down to ownership and copyright considerations, or perhaps they just don't like to share their working file ways (there's always one room to which you keep the door closed when guests come to visit, right?).

There's more about copyright on page 78, but it's worth noting that obtaining the raw, 'working' files may not actually be necessary for every project. If you want to obtain the files to tinker and change things yourself, this is a bigger conversation you might need to have with your designer.

Checklist

ASK FOR BEFORE PROJECT BEGINS

☐ An itemised cost estimate or quote

☐ A project timeline

☐ Copyright ownership and licensing terms

ASK FOR AT THE COMPLETION OF PROJECT

☐ The design in various file formats (with fonts included and/or outlined as appropriate)

☐ Names of typefaces (and where to find them)

☐ Colour breakdowns

☐ Associated images/content that I have rights to use within or outside of the design

Optional extras:

☐ A style guide

☐ Raw design files

NOTES

_____

_____

_____

_____

_____

And that's it.

At this point, my hope is that you're feeling enlightened, empowered, and excited about the potential of your brand-building project. Maybe you've started tapping the keyboard in search of a design partner to assist in your business's next phase… maybe you're going to re-think that email that you were going to send tomorrow to your current designer. Whatever the outcome, knowledge is power, wouldn't you agree?

Keep this book within arm's reach. If you're in the early stages of a project or close to the end, you're going to love the what-to-ask-for list on page 88. If you're in the DIY brand-management phase, it's worth taking a glance at the glossary every now and again for a refresher and to build your business nous.

There is, of course, a lot more to know and learn about graphic design—both creatively and technically. If this book has stirred a longing to know more or even pursue a career in this field, there are lots of entry points: from online tutorials to short courses, all the way through to university degrees.

Finally, forgive me for banging on about this, but when professional goals and money are at stake, it bears repeating: designers are human, just like you. Treat them like you would want to be treated, and trust them like any other professional who has dedicated time, money, and substantial existential effort into their career. If you take steps to speak the same language, you'll have gained an indispensable partner who is both integral to your business success, and cheering you on from the sidelines.

Thank you

Several people were integral to bringing this revised version of *Graphic Design Speak* to life. Editor Emily Rolfe took my words and made them indescribably better in a way only a trained professional can—thank you Emily! Karina Sharpe, Vienna Hawkins and Rebecca Mackey were indispensable as early readers of the text, giving thoughtful feedback about its content (ladies, thank you for being my focus group). Thanks as always to Peter Donoughue and Rose Cuthbertson for their keen eyes at the proofreading stage, and general publishing/life advice. Thank you to Sonya Jeffrey and the team at Books at Manic for helping this book find its readers. And lastly, all the hugs and thanks to my family and friends for their support and encouragement.

REFERENCES

[1] *Owning It: A Creative's Guide to Copyright, Contracts and the Law* by Sharon Givoni, Creative Minds Publishing 2014, page 399
[2] https://en.wikipedia.org/wiki/Copyright accessed 2 May 2019
[3] Givoni, page 376

Index

www.ingramcontent.com/pod-product-compliance
Lightning Source LLC
Chambersburg PA
CBHW040929210326
41597CB00030B/5230